A Tale of Two Bitties

Copyright © 2019 by Jennifer Williams
All rights reserved. This book or any
portion thereof may not be reproduced or
used in any manner whatsoever
without the express written permission of
the publisher except for the use of brief
quotations in a book review.

Printed in the United States of America

First Printing, 2019
ISBN: 9781952422010

Jennifer Williams
Chenoa, IL 61726
AuthorJenniferLush@gmail.com

Preface:

For as long as I can remember, I've said my life is a sitcom, and the only thing missing are the laugh tracks. I believed that funny things just happened to and around me for most of my life. I now understand that it is my sense of humor that creates it. I can experience something with anyone, and our stories about the event will be wildly different because my version with have my out of this world humor embellishing it.

My children were all gifted with my humor, but whether I view this as a blessing or a curse always depends on the day. I am ever thankful for the happy, lighthearted, fun mini-me's I created. They keep laughter in the hearts of all who know them.

At the time I write this, Liz (Boo) is 23, Eric is 12, and Salem (Sally) is 10. They are my everything. I know that is a sentiment that gets used more than picture filters on a smartphone, but they truly are. They are the reason I smile. They are the reason I have peace. They are also the reason I pull my hair out from stress. They are the reason I try to improve myself every single day. If I improve myself, my life will improve which will in turn, improve their lives. They are everything to me and always will be.

I have my own names for the stages of children. You begin life as an itty-itty because you're so tiny. You remain an itty-itty until you are a year old. That's when you become an itty bitty. This stage lasts until about pre-school or 3-4 years old. Bitties are the best. You are a bitty until your 10th birthday. Double digits obviously means you're old. I didn't really have any stages after that because it quickly turns into PTS (Pre Teenager Syndrome) followed by the actual teenage years. My son decided to name this stage mini. In the world according to Eric, PTS doesn't begin until you're 12.

Several years ago I began sharing their comical tales on social media. With every shared antic, people started becoming fans of theirs and my stories about them. So many have encouraged me to write a book. It has taken me awhile to accomplish it. Too long actually, but I have finally finished it. I even have enough material left over for a couple more plus they are generating new comedy gold every single day.

I'm dedicating this book to my mom and dad who were always my biggest fans.

Chapter 1
Bitties on Food

During dinner with Eric (7)...

Me: You're full of beans.
Eric: Nuh-Unh! I don't even eat beans.
Me: Yes, you do.
Eric: No!
Me: You eat green beans.
Eric: Those are NOT beans. They're green.... *realization sank in and he slumped in his chair in disbelief*
September 4, 2013

Sally (5): You know what's funny?
Me: What?
Sally: Cheeseburgers have cheese, but

hamburgers don't have ham.

December 14, 2013

The kids and I went grocery shopping. Liz and I were discussing which salad mix to buy when I noticed Sally (5) was struggling with her arms full several feet away. She had a bag of cut broccoli and cauliflower, a bag of fresh French cut green beans, carrots and celery. I put it all in the cart for her. I helped her and Eric (7) bag cucumbers and bell peppers (green, red, yellow and orange). I asked Sally what kind of tomatoes she wanted, and she picked cherry tomatoes and on the vine tomatoes.

Liz (18): Mom, your kids are spoiled.

Me: Well, if they're spoiled on vegetables, I THINK I can live with that.

February 19, 2014

We all woke up late, and the kids had a late breakfast, no lunch. Sally is getting hungry, but we've been out running errands. Won't be eating till we get home which will be soon. Sally and Liz (18) are arguing over who is hungrier. I decided to butt into the argument.

Me: I've been hungry since I woke up. I haven't ate yet.
Sally (5): Yeah?! Well I've been hungry since I was in your tummy, so no one can say they're hungrier than me right now!
May 4, 2014

Thoughts from the dinner table.

Sally: (5) had a piece of broccoli on her fork.
Sally: Staring contest! *stares at broccoli* You blinked! I win!!

.....

Eric (7): *bites into a cucumber slice*
Mmmm this has really good flavor!
Me: ... Yeah, its cucumber flavored.

.....

Liz (18): *adjusted the blind a couple times because the sun was blinding us*
Eric: The sun is still in my eyes.
Liz: Then delete the sun.
Eric: Pfft. Ok Liz!
Me: Are you in creative?
(Now, for those of you who don't know Minecraft, let me assure you the last one was hilarious!!)
June 5, 2014

Eric (8) decided he wanted biscuits and gravy for dinner even though he hates sausage. Sally (5), having taken the super-secret sibling rivalry oath, must disagree with Eric about everything. This includes what foods they like. When dinner was served, Sally spent 15 minutes explaining to me why she could not possibly eat biscuits and gravy due to having gone to the dentist yesterday. Instead, she ate a plain biscuit and put sausage gravy on her eggs. Meanwhile, Eric had seconds of biscuits and gravy, but wouldn't put gravy on his eggs because 'sausage is gross'.

I never said a word. I just sat and enjoyed the dinner theater.

August 14, 2014

Tonight's dinner theater is brought to you by The Eric and Sally Show! With special guest star, Mom!

Eric was talking about some mashed potatoes he had at someone else's house that were really good.

Sally (5): What made them so good?

Eric (8): *continues talking to me*

Sally: Huh? What flavor were they?

Eric: *continues talking to me*

Sally: What? Were they chocolate flavor or something?

Eric: *stops talking*

.....

Sally: *to Eric* Don't eat the chicken yet. It's still too hot.

Eric: *bites into the fried chicken anyway which by his reaction was still too hot*

Sally: *shakes her head* What'd I tell you Eric?! *sighs*

.....

Eric: Isn't it funny that I like rice cakes, but not rice?

Sally: If you like rice cakes, you like rice. They're made from rice.

Eric: *to me* I think it's because it doesn't taste like rice.

Sally: It tastes like rice! It just feels

different because rice isn't crunchy.

Eric: *to me* Rice is gross, but I liked those rice cake things we had.

Sally: *grunts* Eric! Rice is rice.

.....

Eric: After dinner, can we have pumpkin bread for dessert?

Sally: Yes! Mom already said that.

Eric: Can we mom?

Sally: Eric! Mom said that when it was done. She said we couldn't have any until after dinner.

Eric: Mom?

Me: Yes, after dinner.

Eric: YES!

Me: Why are you ignoring Sally?

Audience Warning: Please lower anything you may be drinking. I can't be held responsible for anyone choking on their drink or suffering from liquids coming out their nose.

Eric: *Throws one hand in the air and rests his head on the other* There's just no talking to her when she's like this mom.

Me: *Stifles immediate swell of hysteria*

Eric: If I talk to her now, we'll just fight. Then I'll have to tell her I'm sorry and I love her and give her a hug.

Me: *Trying not to burst into tears or laughter*

Eric: Ok, mom? I'm just going to wait until she's acting normal again.

Me: *Nods*

August 20, 2014

I went to the store with the bitties. They grabbed a box of cheeseburger macaroni and insisted on having it for dinner. (Who feeds them this stuff?) I told them I could make that if they wanted and didn't need a box to do it. I came home and grabbed the pasta and the Velveeta. My squirrel girl (5) informed me, "um mom....that's TWO boxes."

September 2, 2014

Eric (8): Mom! Thanksgiving is in like 10 days!
Me: I know.
Eric: We got a lot to do then.
Me: *amused* Like what?
Eric: We got a lot to do to prepare.
Me: Ok...like what?
Eric: *opens freezer* You bought a turkey. Did you buy any other food?
Me: Yes, I bought a lot.
Eric: *sigh of relief* Oh, good! I was worried.

Think he's ready to chow?
November 17, 2014

I heated up some Chinese for lunch. Sally (6) wanted the rice, and Eric (8) took the garlic chicken. I ended up with a ham sandwich. Apparently, Sally was picking the peas out of the fried rice and eating them with her fingers. I know this only because I heard Eric tell her to stop doing it because it's gross no less than 14 times while I made my sandwich.

Came to the table. Sat down. Said something to Sally about using silverware. Said something to Eric about not bossing Sally around.

Sally: *starts to reach for a pea with her fingers*
Eric: WHAT DID I JUST SAY?
Both: *turn to me, said sorry, and busted up*
February 21, 2015

Sally talking to her dad about Margaritaville.

Sally (6): I had a cheeseburger in paradise.
James: Was it good?
Sally: Oh yeah. And I ate it like a boss!
April 12, 2015

The bitties made me breakfast in bed. Aww It consisted of a bowl of goldfish crackers, an orange, and a Mountain Dew.

30 minutes later...

Eric (9): When are you making our breakfast?
Sally (6): I want pancakes!

I don't think they quite get the concept yet.
August 22, 2015

I wanted to make orange Jell-O with shredded carrot. Don't judge me. It's one of my favorites. I go to get the carrots out to shred, but no carrots. I search the refrigerator thinking I know I had a bag of carrots in here. Then it hits me. I go to the living room. Sure enough there's two bitties on the couch with an empty bag of carrots. They also had celery and cherry tomatoes. When I asked if there were any carrots left (for my Jell-O), they said no, this is what they wanted for dessert.

Fine by me.
May 4, 2015

Me: What kind of chips did you get?
Eric (8): Potato.
May 22, 2015

Earlier I was making cucumber salad. Cucumbers, onions, apple cider vinegar... Mmmm. The bitties were standing next to me wanting cucumber slices. They watched me put the cucumber in the dish. Then I sliced an onion. ... Put the onion in the dish. ...

Eric (9): Mom! *mortified* You just ruined a perfectly good cucumber!
June 26, 2015

We had Subway, and the bitties had kid's packs. Sally always gets a ham on white, no cheese, tomato, green pepper, cucumber and sometimes pickles. She then opens her sandwich, eats the ham and veggies, and throws away the bread. Every. Single. Time.

Eric (9): Mom says I can order adult meals

whenever I want.

Sally (6): Really?

Eric: Yep. Because I eat all my food. You can't yet because you don't.

Sally: Yes, I do!

Me: *looks at Sally picking apart her sammich* No, you don't.

Sally: I don't like the bread.

Eric: Well, you don't get to eat a big sammich until you actually eat a sammich.

Sally: *holding a green pepper slice in one hand and a tomato slice in the other* I eat it!

Me: No, you pick it apart and eat the toppings. You don't actually eat the sammich.

Sally: But the veggies taste soooo good on their own. I have to eat them separate.

Me: Then why don't you get a salad?

Sally: Because I want a sammich!!!

September 19, 2015

After 26 hours of an anxiety nightmare, I really wanted something sweet, but I'm broke. Looking around the kitchen, I realized I have everything I need to make a no bake cheesecake from scratch. In the words of Sally (6), I'm so glad I don't buy food - I buy "greedients".
September 30, 2015

Sally (7) is helping me finalize the Christmas menu and grocery list. I'm thinking white cheddar mac and cheese and roasted potatoes. Meanwhile, Sally has given me no less 42 different cookie, fudge and truffle ideas as well as chocolate covered marshmallows.
December 12, 2015

Me: *gathering ingredients to make pumpkin bread*

Boo: Whatcha making?
Me: I'm making happy bitties.
December 18, 2015

Leftover night.
Eric (9): I don't want to eat.
Me: You have to eat.
Eric: No, I really don't want anything to eat.
Me: The law says I have to feed you.
Eric: I already ate twice today.
April 25, 2016

My beautiful squirrel (7) made me breakfast in bed. I had crackers, walnuts, and carrots with ranch dressing. I'm not sure if she can't reach the cereal....or just thinks I don't like cereal... Very inventive though. Delicious.
May 8, 2016

Chapter 2
Bitties Take on Medicine

Eric (4): How do babies get out of your stomach?

Me: There's a path they take to come out. "

Eric: Where?

Me: It's under the stomach.

Eric: I wanna see!

Me: You can't.

Eric: Why?

Me: Because it's in my private area.

Eric: *nods knowingly* Oooooohhhhhh....They come out your butt.

May 29, 2011

I woke up this morning (no coffee needed)

to Eric (6) standing by my bed holding a feminine pad and one of Sally's (4) socks.

Me: What are you doing?
Eric: I need help.
Me: *thinking obviously you do* What are you doing?
Eric: Sally has a boo-boo on her foot, and I can't get this in here. *trying to shove pad inside of sock*
Me: Oh...she needs a band aid?
Eric: Yeah, but the Snoopy ones are up to high. These are the only band aids I can reach.
Me: I'll get her a band aid. *takes pad* These aren't band aids.
Eric: Yes, huh! Girls put them in their underwear when they hurt themselves going potty.
February 2, 2013

Driving Sally to Prompt Care for ear infection and sore throat.

Sally: We're close, right?
Me: Yeah. You gonna make it?
Sally: I don't know.
Me: Oh? Please try.
Sally: Alright. Maybe them will say I need to stay a few days.
Me: *grins* I don't think so baby.
Sally: *folds arms across chest* Maybe them will. We'll just have to wait and see.
April 27, 2013

Taking Sally (4) to the doctor earlier...
Sally: (My teacher assistant) is at this doctor.
Me: Really?
Sally: Yeah, (my Pre-K teacher) told us yesterday. She gonna be here for 200 weeks.

Me: Wow. You know that's almost 4 years?
Sally: Yeah, I know, mom. She's pretty bad.
May 15, 2013

Eric (6) left a voice mail for me at work.

"Mom, I fell off the monkey bars at school and ripped my skin off. It's pretty cool."
May 16, 2013

Eric (7): *sneezes*
Liz (17): Bless you.
Eric: *sneezes*
Liz: Bless you.
Eric: *sneezes*
Liz: Bless you.
Eric: Man...I must be coming down with a bad case of the "bless you's", huh?
June 26, 2013

Just like any other siblings, my kids are very competitive. Unlike other siblings, they don't try to compete against each other in sports or school. They don't try to best each other in races, fishing, biking, skating, or anything else. Instead, one can't be sick or injured without another trying to top it. It's like betting; they got to keep raising the ante.

Eric smashes a finger in a door, so Liz breaks her arm at the wrist. Then Sally sits back and says, "alright Liz. I see your broken arm, and I'll raise you a tick bite with illness."

When my little ones' pediatrician retires, I fully expect bids from all the other pediatricians in the county.
July 10, 2013

Poor little bitty! Sally is sick again, so I took Sally and Lucy to see the doctor. She either has croup or bacterial blah blah blah (<--- actual medical term) which is very similar to croup. We're home now armed with bottled water, Jell-O, and popsicles as well as an antibiotic for bacterial blah blah blah and care instructions for croup.
January 27, 2015

Had to run to Prompt Care earlier. Eric has scarlet fever. His 5th or 6th spring in a row to have it. While waiting in the exam room...

Eric (8): *to Sally* Hold your breath, and I'll count how long you hold it for.
Sally (6): OK *takes deep breath*
Eric: 1...2...*groans* You're breathing! My turn. *takes deep breath*

Sally: 12345678910111213141516171819...

Eric: *exhales*

Me: That was like 7, dude.

Eric: You go, mom. Hold your breath, and I'll count.

Me: *Cups hand and blows into it. Closed fingers like a loose fist. Looks at Eric.* Go!

Eric: MOM! I said HOLD your breath!

Me: *lifts hand* I am!

Eric and Sally: *laughing hard*

Eric: That's NOT what I meant when I said that. *continues to laugh then calms down*

Voice Over Robot: Five. Minutes. Later.

Eric: *laughs* Oh my god! Oh! Oh! Oh my! *laughs harder* I told her to hold her breath! *laughs even harder* And she... And she... And she HELD her breath! *beet red, eyes watering, laughing* Oh my

god! She held her breath!
March 17, 2015

Missing the days when the worst part of going to the doctor was looking through the Highlights magazine in the waiting room only to discover someone already found all the hidden objects...and circled them!
March 23, 2015

The absolute fastest way to wake up and get out of bed is hearing the words, "I think I'm going to barf."
October 16, 2015

To anyone who just heard the repeated and heart wrenching "MOMMY NOOOOOO!!" screams, not to worry. I was merely applying peroxide to a boo-boo.

March 8, 2016

Chapter 3
Bitties on Life

What a day. I gave each of the children chores telling them if they did a good job, I'd get pizza during the Super Bowl tomorrow. After I finished cleaning out the fridge, I go check on Eric (6) and Sally (4) who were only told to pick up their room. They were, of course, too busy playing to pick up. I remind them about the pizza.

Sally: Is sissy gonna get pizza even if we don't pick up?
Me: Yes, Liz has been doing what she was told.
Sally: Then, no.
Me: What?
Eric: Yeah, we're not gonna clean.

Me: Why?
Eric: Because mom ... *big ol' grin* ... we're all good sharers, and sissy will share her pizza with us.
Me: *both loving it and hating it at the same time*
Sally: Yeah and I only eat one piece anyway, so sissy will have enough!
February 2, 2013

Eric (6): ... Pfft. I've kissed a girl a million times!
Me: Oh, really?
Eric: Yeah, that's you mom!
February 25, 2013

Told Sally (4) that Papaw is twice my age. I said if you take my age and add it to my age, you have how old Papaw is. Her eyes got huge, and in a soft, awed voice she goes "forty-four." I said that's exactly right, baby. Papaw is 44.

April 27, 2013

Overheard from the living room. The character on TV made one of those comments "if I had (blank) for every time (blank), I'd be (blank)." I didn't quite catch it.

Eric (7): If I had $100 for every time someone said they hated me...
Liz (17): You'd be broke!!!
Mama (Ageless Beauty): *laughed till she had tears*

October 15, 2013

I am so sick of politically correct people ruining the holidays. My kids are each having a "fall party" at school today. Eric (7) brought home a haunted house he made at school, but it's a "fall party"? If it

looks like a vampire, walks like a mummy, and talks like Frankenstein, it's HALLOWEEN.
October 31, 2013

Movie tip for parents: IF you're going to spring for the overpriced popcorn, bring paper lunch sacks for everyone from home. After you buy the tub, distribute the popcorn to the sacks. This way, everyone has their own, and there's no fighting or constant passing (which interrupts the movie with my kids). If you think you need to, pay for the refill before the movie starts, and refill bags when needed. This way you don't miss any of the movie getting more popcorn.
November 3, 2013

Hanging out with the kids, and Eric (7)

and Sally (5) want to know what the word "sexy" means. Hmmmmmmm....

Me: Someone is sexy if you think they're cute, and you want to kiss them.
Sally comes over, and kisses me on the cheek.
Me: Well, it's not a word for family. It's for boyfriends and girlfriends.
Eric: Yeah, you can't marry family.
Sally: *instantly freezes* But, mom...you married dad!

December 12, 2013

You know the old saying/joke about young kids and one can't have a bigger scoop of ice cream than the other? Let's face it. This is true of everything: toys, TV time, etc., and yes, even scoops of ice cream. Sometimes Liz doesn't agree with or understand things I do or allow for the babies. When this happens, I always say, "its scoops of ice cream, Boo. Scoops of ice cream." She immediately knows what I mean.

Apparently, Sally had a banana after school, but Eric didn't. About 20 minutes or so before dinner tonight, Eric asked if he could have a banana.

Liz (18): No.
Eric (7): What? But Sally had one!
Me: *Watching and listening. Waiting to be called into play.*
Liz: I don't care. It'll be dinner time soon. You can't have one right before dinner.
Sally (5): Scoops of ice cream, Boo. Its scoops of ice cream.

How do you argue with that?!
January 29, 2014

Before church, Eric (7) had the broom

holding it across at waist level. He was swinging it around, playing. I told him to put it up. As he turned to put it away, he may have hit Sally (5) with it. There were no witnesses, and Sally didn't have any marks. Sally said it hit her, but Eric said it only came close. He said; she said. Well, Eric put the broom away, and then I heard...

Sally smacks Eric
Eric: Hey! Why'd you do that?!
Sally: Because you hit me with the broom!
Eric: No, I didn't! And you're not supposed to hit back! You're supposed to talk to mom!
Sally: Nuh-uh, Eric, its scoops of ice cream.

Yeah...had to explain a few things after this one.
February 23, 2014

I showed the little babies a pic of me when I was little, and they both thought the girl in the photo was Sally.

Me: Actually that's me.
Sally (5): *face lights up* Really?!
Me: Yeah, don't we look alike?
Sally: That means we're twins! *turns to Liz* Liz, mommy and I are twins!! We just found out!
March 12, 2014

Eric has a teacher who is new this year. Her name is Miss Mills. He really likes her!

Eric (8): Her name isn't going to stay Miss Mills very long.
Me: Oh? She's getting married, huh?
Eric: Yep.
Me: Do you know what her name is going to be after she gets married?

Eric: *looks at me like I'm an idiot* MRS. Mills of course!

August 21, 2014

Eric (8): I wonder who the first person to drink water was. What were their names? ... God made them, but he didn't want them to touch the peach tree. Then they did...

Me: Touched a peach tree? Try ate an apple.

Eric: Oh same thing!

Sally (6): I know! It was Marianne and what was his name?

Me: Marianne?

Sally: Yeah, you know the girl who had the baby.

Eric: Nooooo! That was Jesus' mom.

Me: So Marianne fed her son Jesus a peach? That's what happened?

March 8, 2015

Laptop was open. Eric (9) comes over, and sees a link to an article about Kermit the Frog and Miss Piggy breaking up. He says it out loud and got Sally's (6) attention. They made me read it to them. Afterward, there was shock, disbelief and a lot of asking why.

Finally, Eric looks at Sally and says matter of factly, "well, you know, it's not easy being green."

My heart just burst with love and pride for that little man.
August 9, 2015

Getting the bitties ready for the Cub Scout fishing derby. Told Sally (6) she could use one my poles, but she decided on Eric's old Spiderman pole because it's smaller. Putting a hook on the line, and the pole moves. Sally jumps and screams. I look at her, and she says she scared to death of fishing poles.

Me: You don't have to fish; you can just hang out.
Sally (6): I want to fish.
Me: You're scared of the pole, but you want to fish?
Sally: Once it's in the water I'm not scared. Unless I get a bite. Then I want to drop it and run.

Tomboy she is NOT.
September 27, 2015

The kids were singing "Lucy Says" from the Peanuts (think Simon Says with Lucy's flare.)

Sally (6): And Snoopy won.

Me: Yep, Snoopy beat everyone.

Eric (9): Snoopy can beat everyone at everything except at being a dog. That he'd lose.

October 22, 2015

Chapter 4
Bitties on Growing Up

My little ones were taking turns going to the bathroom, and I heard my 4 year old son tell my 2 year old daughter, "No, baby sissy! If you want to be a BIG kid, you have to stand up to do that!" I didn't know I could move so fast!
May 29, 2011

Me: What do you think of kindergarten so far?
Sally (5): It's just stupid.
Me: Why is that?
Sally: Because you only get one center.
Me: Is there just one center? Or do you only pick one?

Sally: The teacher tells you which center to go to.
Me: What center did you go to?
Sally: I don't know what it's called. *eye roll* There were blocks.
Me: Blocks can be fun.
Sally: I'm an artist! I need colors not blocks!

I think going to the art area every day for two years of Pre-K with her teacher saying that she can tell Sally is going to be an artist when she grows up has her a little spoiled.
August 21, 2014

Sally absolutely hates kindergarten. She told me she had a bad day today. When I asked her about it, she explained that there's too much work to do. All she wants to do is draw, but she has to work all day.
August 22, 2014

Eric (8): *singing* What do I do when I get home from school? I play games, man. I play games, man.

Me: What was that?

Eric: I do homework. I do homework.

Me: Carry on.

Sally (6): *singing* What do I do when I get home from school? I feed the doggy. I feed the doggy.

Me: *singing* What do you do when mom calls your name?

Bitties in Unison: I say yes, mom. I say yes, mom.

Me: I think I like this song.

Eric: It's going to be a hit.

January 20, 2015

Sally wanted to wear shorts today, but it's a little chilly out this morning. Knowing how my diva girl is, I told her to wear pants. She wasn't happy, and refused to get ready for school.

Eric (8): Ugh! Sally! Just get dressed, so we won't be late!
Sally (6): No! Mommy's being mean to me.
Eric: What? How is she being mean?
Sally: I want to wear my new shorts.
Eric: It's cold. ... She wants you to wear jeans. ... So you'll be WARM! ... FIRST WORLD PROBLEMS, SALLY!!

I love them.
April 16, 2015

Sally lost her 3rd tooth tonight. For the third time, after the tooth came out of her mouth, Sally has actually lost her tooth. The tooth fairy is going to get tired of having to go on a treasure hunt through the house to find these teeth.
April 20, 2015

Eric and Sally were teasing and aggravating each other as well as tattling.

Eric (8): Mom! Sally...
Sally (6): Mom! Eric...
...And on and on...
Eric: Mom! Sally lifted her shirt and showed her nipple!
Sally: No, Eric! Yours is nipples. Mine is boobs!
Me: *Nope. Didn't hear any of that.*
June 12, 2015

Sally shot up out of bed this morning at a very unholy hour excited that it was November! Yesterday was Halloween which means today is November! It would be hard for anyone in this home to forget there's a birthday coming up in 2 1/2 weeks.
November 1, 2015

Me: *sobs* (real tears) *sniffle* *sob* That was so beautiful!

Children: *confused*

Me: *continues full body shaking sobbing*

Eric (9): What?

Boo (20): I don't know.

Me: *sobbing* I told Sally (7) to take her bath... And she said, "Okay let me clean up my mess first." *sobs hysterically* I'm so happy!

February 2, 2016

Sally (7): I know how to spell beautiful.

Me: How?

Sally: S-A-L-L-Y

Me: You're so smart!!

February 23, 2016

Eric asked Santa for Madden 17. His dad gave him that game for Christmas last Saturday when he did Christmas with them. I casually asked Eric today what he thought Santa would bring him since he already got the game he wanted. His answer melted my heart!

He thought about it a minute and said, "Well, I'll still get my stocking stuff. Maybe he'll leave me a little something."

No greed. No entitlements. No assumptions. No demands. I love my little man!

December 23, 2016

Chapter 5
Bitties Being Bitties

Sally (3) runs around the house like a banshee for a good 20 min. I tell the kids it's bed time, and she runs to the stairs. She sprawls out over the first 3 or 4 steps. I asked her what she was doing, and she said her batteries just wore out!
June 4, 2012

My darling baby girl decided to use tonight's basketball game to learn how to do cartwheels. Instead of running down the court, she took advantage of the space to practice her future Olympic tumbling routines. My children - entertaining audiences since 1995.
February 12, 2013

Sitting at Denny's, and the kids start talking about when we brought Jaden with us a few months ago. Liz (17) brings up how cute it was that Jaden asked about them and looked for them when the kids left the table.

Eric (6): What? He asked about me?
Me: Yeah, when you used the restroom, he wanted to know where you went. He missed you.
Eric: *smiles big* Yeah...I am a pretty cool kid!
March 3, 2013

Me: Sally (4), you're a goof!
Sally: What the heck?
Me: What was that?
Sally: Hmmmm ... I said is that right?
April 4, 2013
After brushing her teeth for about the 4

billionth time, I said something to Sally (4) about it being past bed time, and she shouldn't be using brushing her teeth repeatedly as an excuse to stay up. Sally told me, "Well, maybe if you quit buying me toothpaste, we wouldn't have this problem!"
June 11, 2013

Last night at the concert, there was a row of porta-potty's about 50 yards from us. The little ones had to go. Sally (4) bypasses the line of about 15-20 people, knocks on each one, even opened the door on some poor soul, and then as soon as one opened, she went in. Afterward, I explained that when there's a line, she needs to wait her turn. She looked up at me and said, "But I REALLY had to pee!"
June 30, 2013

Eric (7): I'm a big fan of race cars.
Sally (4): I'm a big fan of mommy.
Eric: Me too!
Sally: I looooove mommy.
Eric: I love mommy more than Reese's Pieces.
Sally: I love mommy more than Reese's Pieces AND eggs & bacon.
Eric: I love mommy more than Santa Claus.
Sally: .... *silent in defeat*

Eric - 1
Sally - 0
Mommy - So dreading the day when the attitudes kick in, and this ends.
July 12, 2013

Eric writes me a note telling me I'm the best mom he ever had.

Me: And how many moms have you had?
Eric (7): A lot!
Me: ... In THIS lifetime?
Eric: One, but I don't want anyone else!

May 19, 2014

Eric (8): *laying on floor, grabbing his feet*
Me: What are you doing?
Sally (5): He's pretending to be a mouse.
Eric: Squeak. Squeak.
Me: I've never seen a mouse grab his feet before.
Sally: I know! See something new all the time! Lucky day, right?

August 12, 2014

I got up this morning and woke up the bitties. Went back to my room and sat against the headboard checking my phone. Eric comes flying into my room.

Eric (8): Mom! We got school!

Me: I know. Get dressed.

Eric: I am. Just waking you up.

Me: *laughs* I am awake. I woke you up.

Eric: *freezes in mid stride* You woke me up?

Me: *laughs harder* Yes.

Eric: When?!

Me: When did you wake up?

Eric: *confused* What? I'm asleep.

August 22, 2014

Eric (8) bursts into my room this morning yelling that we overslept and missed the bus. I jumped up, put on just enough clothing to be able to leave the house without facing indecent exposure charges, and ran downstairs. No kids. I'm about to yell upstairs for them to hurry when I glance at the clock. 4:53 am. I walk upstairs and go into Eric's room who was back asleep in bed. Opening his bedroom door woke him up, and he yells out mad that he's trying to sleep. This is going to be a long school year...

August 29, 2014

At dinner earlier, Sally was showing off about being able to speak Spanish.

Sally (5): Hola! That means hello. Adios! That means goodbye.

Silence

Eric (8): Just because you can say two words doesn't mean you know how to speak Spanish.

Sally: *In an "I'll show you" attitude* JOSE!!

That's my girl.

October 20, 2014

"Don't worry guys. I'm undivisible." ~ Sally Rose Williams (6)

December 28, 2014

Sally's (6) rendition of Taylor Swift's "22":
"It feels like a perfect night...to dress up like hamsters."
January 2, 2015

BAD BITTIES!!

Eric (8) and Sally (6) were quiet the entire drive home from town which is unusual. As we got into Chenoa, I joked with them about if I had any bitties.

Me: Do I still have bitties in the backseat? *Silence*
Me: Eric? *Silence* Sally? *Silence* Huh, I wonder what happened to my bitties. Eric, are you here?
Eric: Yeah.
Me: *laughs* I was beginning to wonder what happened to my bitties. Is Sally here?

Eric: Nnn-nnn NOOOO! MOOOOOMMMMMM!!!!!
Me: *Heart stops and whip my head around to see Sally ducked down smiling* DUDE! That's not even funny!
Eric: *laughing* Yeah, dude. It kinda was!
January 8, 2015

Sally (6) comes home and begins telling me all about what she's going to do from now on. She grabs the broom and starts sweeping (wasn't told to). Sally spends a good 10 minutes going on about how she's going to behave, listen and do what she's told. She's going to do more chores and clean the whole house by cleaning a different room every day. She's going to be a big help to me and will always be on the "nice list".

I listen to my beautiful baby girl describe

every mother's utopia to me. Just waiting. I knew "it" was coming. I figured for being a full time maid with the behavior of a saint, she must be wanting Disney. I knew something was coming; I just didn't plan on it being Eric.

Out of nowhere, Eric (8) walks in the room, and says, "Yeah, yeah, yeah. Just wait till tomorrow when you're all *whiny/fussy voice* but I don't want to set the table! I want to color and watch Frozen. You're mean, mom!"

Oh, god bless them both.
January 12, 2015

Eric (8) brought the book "Captain Underpants and the Perilous Plot of Professor Poopypants" home from school. I notice he looks very interested in it.

Me: Good book?

Eric: Yes. I'm on 7 now, but when I started, I was only on level 2.

Me: Chapter 2.

Eric: Huh? What?

February 10, 2015

Yesterday, I told my bitties I thought we should go to Disney instead of NYC for vacation. Because A) if I'm going to take them to Disney, I'd like to do it when they're young, and B) if I'm going to take them to NYC, I'd like to do it when they're a bit older.

This news was not received well. I "broke their hearts". (That's Sally's newest favorite phrase.)

Nooooooooo!

I don't want to go to Disney!

Disney is just stupid people dressed up in costumes!

I want to see the Empire State Building lit up at night.

I want to go to the Statue of Liberty.

I want to go to the biggest Toys R Us and the big Macy's.
Followed by pouts and cries.

They even said I could go to Disney, and they'd stay with Papaw who'd take them to NYC because Papaw takes them anywhere they want.

Today, I told them I booked our vacation. They asked what I meant. I said I booked our room and bought tickets.

Eric (8): Where?

Me: Florida.

Eric: Disney?

Me: Well, yes. Disney. Universal. Sea World.

Eric: So, wait... We're going to Disney?

Me: Yes.

Eric and Sally share a look and smiles start to form.

Eric: So...we're really going to Disney?

Me: Yes.

bigger grins

Eric: So...Disney? We're going to Disney?

Me: Yes. *laughs*

Squeals of delight from the bitties

What a difference a day makes!

February 12, 2015

The bitties and I have been watching the Harry Potter movies which they're handling much better than Honey, I Shrunk the Kids. (Yeah, they make about as much sense as I do.) Tonight we watched the 5th movie, Order of the Phoenix. There's a scene where the students are taking the OWL test, and Fred & George come flying in on broomsticks setting off fireworks. They chase Umbridge out of the room with them, and the crazy amount of rules that are posted on the walls outside the door come crashing down and break on the floor.

Eric (8): And now...*cool announcer voice* They've broken ALL the rules!
Me: *laughs* Good one.
Eric: Did you get it mom?
Me: *laughing* Yeah, baby. You made a funny. A good one.
February 17, 2015

Sally (6) was walking out of the living room. Eric (8) was hiding around the corner.

Eric: Boo!
Sally: *jumps and yells*
...
Sally: Slow motion!

They resume their positions and reenact the scare several times at snail speed. The most interesting part is just how entertaining it is to watch.

February 27, 2015

Sally (6): Does Eric have a soccer ball game tonight?
Eric (8): It's just soccer, not soccer ball.

Later...

Sally: What time is it? Is it time for Eric's soccer ball?
Eric: Sally! It's just soccer. Not soccer BALL!

Later...

Eric: Sally! Come on! It's time for my soccer ball game!
April 16, 2015

Eric (8): I can't wait till tomorrow!
Me: Why?
Eric: Because I get better looking every day!

Takes after me
April 24, 2015

Sally (6) is such a morning person just like me. Haha After crying, complaining, carrying on, asking for one minute, saying she's awake but stretching only to be asleep again a minute later, and all the other dramatics we go through every morning, Sally finally gets up.

Sally: *sneezes*
Me: Bless you.
Sally: *sneezes*
Me: Bless you.
Sally: Are you going to stop that?!
Me: Stop what?
Sally: Making fun of me!
Me: I'm not making fun of you.
Sally: *crying* You are!
Me: How?
Sally: You're making fun of me sneezing.
Me: ... *confused* Saying bless you? That's polite, not making fun.
Sally: *goes into different room crying*
...
Sally: (from the kitchen) *sneezes*
Eric: Bless you.

Sally is now in her room. Crying. Claiming

that we hate her and make her feel bad.

I feel sorry for the man she marries one day...
May 4, 2015

(Bloomington-Normal are twin cities in central IL. My brother lived in Normal, IL at the time of this conversation with my young sarcasm protégé.)
This afternoon in the car...

Eric (8): We haven't been to Bloomington in a really long time.
Me: You just went.
Eric: No.
Me: Twice.
Eric: No.
Me: This week.
Eric: *shakes head no*
Me: To Uncle Rick's.

Eric: That's Normal. *grins*

He was on a roll today.

May 22, 2015

I have a little decoration in my kitchen that reads "A messy kitchen is a sign of happiness". Sally read it, and said, "Our kitchen is messy. A little bit."

Me: Are you happy?
Sally (6): Yes!
Eric (8): No.
Me: Why not?
Eric: Because the kitchen is messy.

June 17, 2015

Sally (6): *singing*

Jingle bells

Jingle bells

Jingle all the way

Jingle bells

Jingle bells
Jingle with delight
I can't remember all the words
On this summer night
Hey!
July 25, 2015

The bitties are making paper necklaces. They decided to make one for me. Eric (9) measured around my neck for the fit, but then I couldn't look because it was a surprise. They sat on my bed coloring and cutting and taping. Finally, I hear...

Sally (6): *to Eric* There! What do you think?
Eric: I don't know.
Sally: It's a heart because mom loves us, and we love her.
Eric: But it's not good enough. Not for mom anyway. We can do better.

Sally: Yeah...bigger...and with stickers!

They melt me.
August 7, 2015

Sally (6): Can we watch a movie?
Me: No, it's already past bedtime.

30 minutes later...

Sally: Can we watch a movie to fall asleep?
Me: No, close your eyes and be still to fall asleep.

10 minutes later...

Sally: Can we watch a movie real fast?
Me: How you gonna do that? Watch it in fast forward?
September 14, 2015

Today's homework assignment is to describe a day spent as a butterfly. Sally (6) wrote one sentence.

Me: You can write more than that.
Sally: I can't think of anything.
Me: If you woke up tomorrow as a butterfly, what's the first thing you would do?
Sally: Go back to sleep.

Fair enough.
November 11, 2015

Talking to Boo about the bitties...
Me: They're my twins born 2 years apart.
Eric (9): Noooo!
Me: Sorry. But it's true.
Sally (7): I don't want to be his twin!
Me: It don't matter. You two look just alike. I think you were meant to be twins,

but Sally was just on backorder or something.

December 22, 2015

I woke up this morning to...

Eric (9): Mom, I don't have any clean jeans.
Me: This is not the sort of thing you tell me so close to school starting.
Eric: *moans and groans*
Me: Wear sweats. I know you have clean sweat pants.
Eric: What?! NO! I'm not wearing sweats to school!
Me: Wear pajamas then. I'm doing laundry today. You'll have clean jeans tomorrow.
Eric: *groans and leaves room*
5 minutes later Eric walks into the living room wearing clean jeans
Me: Where'd you find those?

Eric: Huh?
Me: In your dresser?
Eric: *stares blankly* What?

And I thought my memory was getting bad.
April 4, 2016

Eric (9) had a poor attitude, so I sent him to his room to clean which didn't exactly help his attitude any. After a few minutes, he asked if I would help fix the sheet on his bed. I did. As I left the room, I kissed his head and told him I love him. He said, "I love you too. You're still the best mom in the world even if I am mad at you."
April 11, 2016

At Dollar General, I open my purse and pull out a pair of orange plastic TMNT

nunchucks. After the laughter over my confused and humored expression dies down, "I'm really not trying to rob you. I'd have brought a better weapon if I was."
April 19, 2016

The bitties sometimes get identical shirts for sports teams or whatever. Their names are written on the tags, so we can tell them apart. Liz was helping to fold laundry and pulled out a bitty sports shirt. The name on the tag was so faded she couldn't read it.
Sally (7): Let me see that! ... It belongs to 50% cotton....

Lolololol I couldn't stop laughing.
April 22, 2016

There was some commotion in the house

not long ago because apparently Sally called Eric a B(utt) H(ole.) Very unusual of Sally, but I talk to Sally about what she said then it's Eric's turn.

Me: What were you doing RIGHT before Sally (7) called you a BH?
Eric (9): Getting ready.
Me: No. What were you doing to SALLY right before she called you a BH?
Eric: I took her crossword away from her. (This is a MAJOR offense in Sally's world. I thought well that does explain things.)
Me: Why did you take her crossword?
Eric: She was supposed to be getting ready.
Me: ... Did I tell you to take her crossword away?
Eric: No, but you told me to tell her to get ready.
Me: Telling her to get ready doesn't include taking her crossword.

Eric: *puts hand across his heart* Mom...I do what I got to do.

So precious yet so ornery.
April 29, 2016

Off to the 1st grade field trip to the Planetarium. Eric is mad because I'm missing his luau.
A) I went to the Planetarium with him when he went.
B) I went on his Springfield field trip with him this year.
C) I was at his Christmas luau.

I can't win! Lol
May 20, 2016

Eric (9): *on computer in different room*
Sally (7): I'm going to Eric's room to watch

videos.

Me: Okay. I'm going to watch a show where people get killed then.

Eric: *from other room* You say that like it's a good thing.

Me: ... You say that like you're surprised.

May 22, 2016

I don't get the newspaper regularly, but I bought one last Sunday. Sally (7) picked up the comics and said, "Look, mom! The Peanuts made the news!"

June 15, 2016

Sally (7): *singing* I'm so bored. Bored. Bored. B-bored.

Me: I said I was going to drink my coffee before we leave.

Sally: *looks in my mug* That'll take forever! I could die!

Me: Then I won't have to buy your school supplies and save me a little money.

Sally: *GROWLS* That is NOT helping!

August 13, 2016

So I'm writing "Sally W." on all of Sally's school supplies... You know... Because that last initial is needed to identify her from all the other Sally's?

August 14, 2016

Open House for Sally later...

Sally (7): *Checks for umbrella*
Me: We should put your book bag in a trash bag to bring over, so all your new stuff doesn't get soaked.
Sally: Dude! ...that's actually a pretty good idea.
Me: Thank you. Glad you approve.

August 15, 2016

I think Eric (10) and Sally (7) are tired.

Sally: *walks in from car carrying floor mat*
Me: Need that for something?
Sally: Yeeeesss.
Me: Like what?
Sally: What?
Me: The floor mat.
Sally: *looks down with obvious surprise and confusion*
Me: Drop it down. I'll get it.
Eric: *walking toward house with one shoe on*
Me: Where's your shoe?
Eric: What?
Me: You're missing a shoe.
Eric: I don't know!
Me: And that shoe is on the wrong foot.
August 19, 2016

Me: How did you get so handsome?
Eric (10): I don't know.
few seconds pass
Eric: Wait! I know. Because I got my looks from you.
Me: Oh! I love you!
August 28, 2016

We were looking for the base to my phone charger, and Boo finds a lidded storage container of water under my bed.

Boo (20): What's this?
Me: I don't know...Sally (7)?
Boo: But why?
Me: I don't know. *takes a closer look* She put holes in the lid. She must have caught something. What's in there?
Boo: Nothing.
Me: Are you sure? It's probably dead. Floating.
Boo: Nothing.

Me: Great. It's escaped. Probably hiding behind my head board, hungry and gonna devour me in my sleep.

August 31, 2016

Me: You need to brush your hair.
Sally (7): *growls* I can't! It's impossible!
Me: See if Boo will help you.
Sally: *feigns death on the couch*
Me: I still have to get ready. See if Boo will help you.
Sally: She probably doesn't even have a brush! I'm going to walk all the way over there, and she's just gonna send me back for one!
Me: Just take. The brush. With you. Don't make this harder than it is.
Sally: She's gonna kill me and pull out all my hair!
Me: Well...at least you won't feel it then.

September 7, 2016

Eric (10): Can I get on the computer?

Me: It's 6:38 in the morning.

Eric: Yeah...there's time before we have to go.

Me: You want to use the computer?

Eric: *laughs* Yes.

Me: At 6:38 in the morning?

Eric: *laughs* Yes.

Me: I don't even know how to spell my name at 6:38 in the morning!

September 7, 2016

Eric (10): Can I get on the computer?

Me: Is your room clean?

Eric: What?! I have to have that WHOLE room clean first?!

Me: Nah...just the bottom half.

October 7, 2016

Eric cleaned his room today.

Me: Dude, I don't want to alarm you, but

there's some ginormous brown thing on the floor of your room. I've never seen anything like it before.

Eric (10): *runs to his room* Where? *steps inside*

Me: Watch out! It'll eat your feet!

Eric: *rolls eyes* I can't believe I fell for that.

Me: *confused* What is it?!

Eric: Carpet, mom. It's my carpet.

October 10, 2016

Eric (10): *Wakes up and comes into my room seemingly surprised to see me.*

Me: What's wrong?

Eric: Nothing. *Sits next to me. Snuggles for a minute.*

Me: What's wrong?

Eric: Nothing.

Me: Then why aren't you in bed?

Eric: I was looking for the thing.

Me: What thing?

Eric: The suit thing.

Me: *hmmmmm* Can we look for it in the morning?

Eric: Yeah.

Me: Okay. You look handsome in a suit.

Eric: *nods*

Wonder what he was dreaming.....

October 10, 2016

Eric (10): If you type 666 into your phone, will the devil answer?

Me: No. There's no cell phone reception in hell.

November 21, 2016

Boo is trying to mop the kitchen which of course means Eric and Sally have to come in the kitchen right now! Sally is starving and dying of thirst even though 42 seconds ago, she was absolutely fine.

Me: Boo is mopping! You can wait! No one is going to die in the next 10 minutes!
Sally (8): Yes, I AM!!
Me: Then I will buy you really beautiful flowers for your funeral. I promise!!
December 18, 2016

Chapter 6
Sibling Love

Sally wanted to sing a song, but wanted someone to tell her what to sing.

Eric: I know! I got one.

Sally: *folds arms over chest and rolls eyes* No, Eric. I'm not wanting to listen to boys right now!

March 28, 2013

Eric (6) and Sally (4) were arguing.

Eric: Look. I'm older than you. I know stuff.

April 3, 2013

Earlier tonight at the store, Eric (7) and Sally (4) were disagreeing.
Eric: I'm really getting tired of her!
Me: *busts up laughing*
Eric: Mom! It's not funny. I'm serious.
Me: *still busting up laughing* I know you're serious, honey. That's what makes it so funny.
July 4, 2013

During dinner, Sally (5) suddenly started screaming and jumped up running across the kitchen. "SPIDER!!" It was a daddy long legs. A baby one. Actually, it was more like a newborn, just climbed out of the egg sac daddy long legs. Eric (7) starts screaming too and runs in the other room. I go look, but I don't see it anywhere.

Sally: KILL IT!!
Me: Where is it?!

Eric: KILL IT!!
Me: I don't see it!

I fully intended on finding it and taking it outside as I always do. (Spider relocation program.) But I honestly did not...see...anything! By now, both my kids are in a panic. Sally is moments away from a full blown meltdown. Their frenzy is causing me to panic because I know if I want to restore order in my home, I must find this spider that I wasn't even sure existed at this point.

Eric: It's on the chair!
Me: *looks at chair* Where?!
Eric: Right there!!
Me: *throws hands up* I don't see it!
Sally: *shaking and sobbing violently in the corner*
Eric: *comes into the kitchen, shoe in hand, and I finally see the spec of a spider

a nanosecond before he kills it*

He then goes over to Sally and puts his arms around her. He kisses her head and reassures her over and over again that it's okay now. She's safe. The spider is dead, and it was a daddy long legs anyway. They're not really dangerous. He stood there holding her for at least a good 3 minutes until she calmed down.

I LOVE HIM!! He's always making me so proud!
June 7, 2014

I was telling Boo that once Eric goes to UE for 5th grade, he won't be in the same school as Sally again until he's a senior in high school.

Liz (19): *to Eric* You better protect her.

Eric (8): Why?

Liz: Because high school is scary.

Sally (6): No. I'm going to have to protect him.

June 5, 2015

Liz and Eric have been playing/teasing/annoying each other for a while. Liz runs upstairs. Eric runs after her. Eric comes halfway back down the stairs laughing hysterically.

Eric (8): Mom, can I have a fork?

Me: For what?

Eric: You do NOT want to know!

June 5, 2015

Last night, Eric and Sally built a fort in the living room. I was so impressed with how week they worked together, communicated, and complimented each other.

This morning, they were arguing about a monster game Eric plays. Every time the argument would die down, one of them would make a remark to stir it up again.

Such good siblings! Lol
June 16, 2015

Eric (9) is adorable. He picked out coloring books and crayons for his sister at the store. He carefully put them where she will find them on her own. Eric wrote a note in his best handwriting, so Sally (6) won't know it was him telling Sally to enjoy, signed Dora.
September 11, 2015

Sally (6): I wish I had a twin. You know why?

Me: To drive mommy crazy.
Sally: No. It's because it would... Wait. Hey!
Eric (9): *laughs*
Sally: No. Eric already has that covered.
September 24, 2015

Sally has words that she has to be able to read each week. They're called word wall words. Sally always does well. This week they're reviewing the words from the first 9 weeks. There are 63 of them. She took the paper from her book bag tonight and groaned. She had so many words to do! Eric immediately said he'd help her review them. I love my bitties.
November 2, 2015

Eric (9): Can I have one of the folders from the extra school supplies?

Me: Yes.

Eric: *gets folder* I want to write "Sally's Pretty Pictures" on it and decorate it with stickers because she's always drawing and coloring. Then she can put her pictures in here when the fridge has no more room.

Me: That's awesome.

Eric: Will you help me wrap it?

Me: Of course!

Eric: *showing me the folder when he's done* Do you think she'll like it?

Me: Honey that is the most thoughtful gift that's gonna be under our tree this year. She's going to love it!

December 20, 2015

Chapter 7
Lessons Learned

After talking to Eric (6) and Sally (4) about getting into things without permission...
Eric: ...but I didn't.
Sally: Yes.
Eric: No, you did! Not me!
Sally: *stands straight and puts hands on her hips* Yes!
Eric: Nuh-uh! *runs into living room*
Sally *runs after him and shakes finger at him* YES! You did! We BOTH did!
Eric: NO! It was YOU!
Sally: *picks up TV remote and turns off TV then shakes remote at Eric* No more TV for you, brother, until you learn to stop lying!
Me:*leans against counter watching the

whole thing eating Special K crackers like it's popcorn at a theater*
January 25, 2013

That moment when you realize you need to watch what you say in front of your children.

Liz and I were on the back porch talking. Sally opened the door and said, "keep it down. I can hear you. For cryin' out loud!"
July 08, 2013

I came home from work today with a brand new box of Crayola. Sally took the page I colored with her to bed. Ain't nothing tops the feeling of knowing you made your child feel special.
August 30, 2013

I just got home from taking Liz to work. I unlocked the door. Eric opened it and said, "after you mom." I went inside, and Eric looked at Sally sort of nodding for her to go in. Sally was pouting, and said she wanted to open the door. She came inside, and I told her that men are supposed to open the door for ladies.

Eric (7): "Yeah. I'm a man, and you're the lady. You're supposed to let me do things for you. It's kinda like my job."

Could my heart melt anymore??
April 27, 2014

The Pre-K field trips always end at the mall. I took Sally shopping and bought her a few things. When we were done, we went outside to wait for the bus. Two other boys and parents were already outside.

Sally (5): *to one of the boys* Do you want to see what I got? *proceeds to start pulling lip gloss and jewelry from her bags*

Boy: ... No.

Boy's Dad: Go ahead and let her show you.

Boy: *looks at dad like why do you hate me?*

Boy's Dad: Be a sport and see what she got.

Way to go dad! That's how you teach the kid young how to act around a lady!

May 23, 2014

This morning I'm in the kitchen attempting to make my first cup of coffee which is especially dangerous because I don't have the required caffeine level yet necessary to operate even small kitchen appliances when I hear a frantic, "MOM!

Quick!" I turn, lose my balance, catch myself, stumble over a kitchen chair, crash into the fridge, right myself again, and wander in the direction of my son's voice.

I find Eric (8) standing in his bedroom doorway. He says, "Look!" *turns off bedroom light with a big grin on his face* "I figured it out! Huh? Turn the switch DOWN, and the light goes OFF. Huh? Right? I did good."

That kind of sarcasm makes me proud, but he obviously went back into his room this morning. I still had to turn his bedroom light off after taking the bitties to school. He tried...
October 28, 2014

Eric was in a mood tonight and was kind

of mean to his sister a couple of times. Then he did it again. Called her a "dummy".

Me: Eric, what did I just tell you?
Eric (8): What?
Me: We are not mean in this house.
Eric: No, you said we are not mean in this house for no reason. I had a reason. She is a dummy.
December 27, 2014

Poor, poor Eric...He hasn't learned yet that if you call me "the worst mom ever", I will accept the challenge.
January 3, 2015

The bitties and I were unloading the car. Eric (8) didn't have anything in his hands.

Me: Is that all of it?
Eric: All that's left is a bag with trash in it.
Me: Get that bag too.

God bless my boy...

I turn around and see Eric running up to me with an empty bag in hand just a blowing in the wind. The trash was on the floor board. *sighs*
January 10, 2015

Lesson learned.

While grocery shopping on Saturday, I let the bitties pick out a package of donuts. I very rarely buy donuts. Past donut experiences consistently have one or both bitties waking up early and eating all or almost all of them. They then lay around all day complaining their belly hurts. I wonder why. If only one bitty gets into the donuts, the other bitty is upset and in a sour mood all day.

I thought I could prevent this, and it worked. Sort of. Saturday evening they asked if they could have donuts in the morning. I told them yes, but not until I was awake.

Guess who woke up at 6 am Sunday morning to two bitties and a box of donuts being held 2 inches from her face? SIX!! A.M!! They don't wake that early on Christmas!! Mom. Mom. Mom. Mom. Mom. Mom. Mom. Mom. Donuts?

Last night, they asked if they could have donuts again this morning. I said yes. We wake at 6 during the week anyway. FIVE!! That's right! 5 am, and I have two bitties with a box of donuts in my face! Mom.

Mom. Mom. Mom. Mom. Mom. Mom. Mom. Donuts?

My son set his alarm an HOUR early to make sure they had time to eat a donut for breakfast.

I am NEVER buying donuts again!
January 26, 2015

I was watching a show where a character said something along the lines of 'I hated him, but I didn't want anything bad to happen to him.'

Eric (8): The bible says you shouldn't hate your enemies.
Me: What does that mean?
Eric: It means don t hate them, and don't do mean things back to them, and you should pray for them.

Me: *heart melted twice in one day* I am so thankful for you.

April 17, 2015

Coming home from the Cub Scout food drive...

Eric (8): I don't know why I said no when I was asked if I wanted to be in charge.
Me: Ah well. Don't worry about it.
Sally: You could've been in charge?
Eric: I told her no.
Sally: Why?!
Eric: Because I just...got my own opinions on life.

May 9, 2015

I have a magnetized can opener that is always put on the top right of the fridge. Earlier I asked Eric (8) to get me the can opener off the front of the icebox. He didn't know what an icebox was. I was amused, so I asked Sally (6). They spent 15 minutes searching. They really thought the icebox was the deep freezer. Finally, Eric said wait...it's where the ice is! And found it. I was cracking up watching them.

May 25, 2015

Sally (6) calls highways "high roads".

Sally: Why did we turn on this high road?
Eric (9): It's not the high road. Just a regular road that's bigger.
Me: The road I'm on is always the high road.
Eric: .... What?
Me: Remember it when you're older.

August 17, 2015

I love all these posts from people who hate

the time change. I love this time change!! I love that it gets dark earlier!! I can send my bitties to bed at 6:30. They have no idea it's 1 1/2 hours before bedtime... Lol
November 1, 2015

Sally decided to have her first ever tea party today. She gave all of us invitations yesterday and made sure we RSVP'ed. After school, she started to get ready for it, so I offered to help. I began by making tea, and Sally grabbed cups from the cabinet.

Me: Those are the wrong cups.
Sally (7): Which ones do we use?
Me: I'll get the cups. You worry about what we're having with the tea.
Sally: What do you mean?
Me: Usually there are tea biscuits, but we don't have any. Find something we can use instead.

Sally came back to the table with a box of Ritz crackers while I was setting the teacups and saucers down.

Sally: Those are your special dishes!
Me: Yes, they're called china.

We also filled the china sugar bowl for the occasion. Eric walks in, eyes widen, looks from the table to the china cabinet.

Eric: Mom? We never use these.
Me: They're for SPECIAL occasions only.
Eric and Sally: *exchange glances*

We had a lovely tea. Polite conversation about school and Santa's workshop. We made sure to raise our pinkies as much as possible. When I was cleaning up, I heard Eric tell Sally, "Mom REALLY loves us."

They're still talking about it. Moral of the

story: It never costs a dime to make your bitties feel loved.

February 1, 2016

Its daddy's visit day, and James agreed to take Eric to get his haircut because our weekends have been filled with other activities lately. So nice of him. I just got a text from James that said, "Sally's hair looks cute." I'm worried. Should I be worried? Where are my anxiety meds? I need a drink.

April 27, 2016

Chapter 8
Lucy Doll Chronicles

So this is an old story, but one that seems to be coming up in conversation a lot lately. I thought I'd share.

A couple Christmas' ago, Sally (then 4) got one of those doll accessories kits. The kind that has a bassinet, stroller, high chair, etc. Every night after that for months, the doll and bassinet were in my room by my bed. Even though I had to work in the morning and Sally had afternoon pre-k, her baby doll slept in my room, so I could get up during the night to feed her because Sally needed her sleep.

Oh, I know! How sweet, huh? Adorable,

right?

Every night she'd put the doll to bed in my room. In the morning, I'd take the doll to her room, wake her up, and give her the doll to care for because I had to go to work.

Yes. This is what my mommy life had become. Taking care of my baby's doll.

Until one night...I woke up around 4am to a very angry bitty. Sally was scolding me because I slept through her baby's cries. Sally heard them and was woke up all the way in her room (across the hall), and I slept through it.

I was never allowed to babysit again. Still. To this day. The doll fends for herself while Sally is gone. I'm not allowed. All because I didn't wake up to the imaginary cry of a doll. Once.

This is just a small window into the world I live in every day.

November 9, 2014

Sally (6) has a baby doll named Lucy, and Sally is a very good mommy to her baby. Eric's favorite saying lately is, "ugh she's not real!"

During Christmas dinner, Lucy was in her baby doll high chair that James gave Sally for Christmas. Sally got a bowl of food just for her baby, and would regularly feed her.

Eric (8): Why does Sally have that bowl?

James (age too high to count): It's food for her baby.

Eric: So Sally gets two dinners?!

James: *laughs* No, Sally has her plate and a bowl of food for her baby.

Eric: *matter of fact tone* I saw Sally eat food from that bowl. It's not for her baby.
James: Newsflash, Eric. *quietly whispers* Lucy is a doll. She's not going to eat that food.

December 26, 2014

My bitties each received a Christmas card with $5 in it a couple weeks ago. We went to the store, and Eric (8) bought Pokemon cards, of course. Sally (6) bought a stuffed unicorn for her baby doll Lucy that we wrapped and put under the tree for Christmas because Lucy loves unicorns. (FYI, Sally does not.)

Meanwhile, this baby of Sally's has no accessories. Nothing. Sally was wrapping the doll up in a towel as a blanket until I gave her my scarf to use.

So as I was finishing up getting what I needed for Christmas, I came across a nursery bedding design that was reduced because the store wasn't going to carry it anymore. A baby blanket for $2. Yes, I bought it for Lucy doll. Yes, I wrapped it and put it under the tree.

My first gift I ever bought for a grandbaby was for a doll. And I wrapped it. Tagged it to Lucy from Memaw. And I put it under the Christmas tree.

Now you know I've seriously lost my dang mind.

December 26, 2014

The Lucy Doll Chronicles: Episode 3

During the drive home tonight, Sally started talking about Lucy which really upset Eric because "it's a doll!" Then Sally mentioned that she believed her baby (doll) was old enough to do chores now.

Eric (8): Ugh! It's a doll!
Me: Don't irritate your sister.
Sally (6): Right mom? She can do chores.
Me: I'm sure we can find a chore for her to do.
Eric: Mom! It's a DOLL!
Me: Don't irritate your sister.
Eric: How is that irritating her?
Me: Because you're saying something you know will upset her.
Eric: *flabbergasted* But! It's a doll! Mom! Tell her.
Me: I'm not telling her anything.
Eric: *to Sally* Fine. Give her chores. It'll just be you doing extra chores anyway.

2 miles down the road.....

Sally: Mom, Lucy really loves the blanket you gave her. It's so warm.

Eric: *sing songy* It's a doll!

Me: Eric, stop.

Eric: But it is. A doll.

Sally: She's my baby.

Eric: No. It's not. It's. A.....doll.

100 yards farther.....

Sally: When are we going to have dinner? Lucy is really hungry.

Eric: *whispers with a facepalm* Oh my god! It's a doll!

Me: *Laughed the rest of the drive home.*
December 26, 2014

We were sitting down to dinner last night just about to say grace when Sally remembered that Lucy now has a high chair. She jumped up to get it. Eric started to object, but I told him to wait a minute. Sally brings the high chair over and puts Lucy in it. We say grace, and I asked Eric what was his complaint.

Eric (8): I share all my toys with Sally. Even my most specialist toys that are my favorite. If she wants to play with them, I let her.
Me: *very confused*
Eric: She won't let me play with Lucy! Not ever!
Me: You want to play with her baby?
Eric: Yes!!! She won't let me!
Me: *I thought it was JUST a DOLL!!*
Sally: Well, it's just that after dinner, I have to work on her learning stuffs. We have to do her numbers and her letters.
Me: Why don't you let Eric help? Let him do Lucy's numbers.
Sally: Weeeeellllll..... He'll probably do

something silly like 1...40, and Lucy won't learn then.

Me: Give him a chance, Sally. See how he does.

Sally: *to Eric* Maybe you can do her colors.

Eric: No, I can do her numbers.

Me: *Tunes out the conversation at this point still lost in the surprise that Eric's problem with Lucy doll all along was that he wanted to play with her, but wasn't allowed to. Tunes back in upon hearing the word "app".*

Me: What app?

Eric: I'm going to download a learning app to help Lucy learn her words and numbers and colors and stuff. That's a good idea isn't it?

Me: Yes, it is. *Whole dang family lost their minds!*

December 27, 2014

Finally, I can go to sleep. Why am I up so late? I'm glad you asked. Sally (6) took Lucy doll into the bathroom tonight when she took a bath even though I told her not to. Yes, Lucy who is part cloth got soaked. It took forever to get her dry. Sally went to bed in tears because she didn't have her baby doll, so I promised her that as soon as Lucy was dry, I'd bring her up. Lucy dried. I swaddled her in her blanket. Then tucked Lucy and Lucy's stuffed unicorn into bed next to Sally.

The things I do...
January 4, 2015 12:36am

I have been redeemed!!

Earlier Sally asked out of the blue if I'd like to have Lucy Doll stay with me tonight.

I brought it up later, and Sally said well maybe Lucy can spend some time with you before you bring her up to me.

When Sally went to bed, I didn't even mention it. Sally came down a little bit ago with Lucy Doll, and told me Lucy really wanted to stay the night with her grandma!

January 7, 2015

I keep forgetting to post this. Sally (6) came home sick on Wednesday. I took her to the doctor on Thursday, and she had strep throat. She's better now.

While we were at her appointment, Sally's doctor gave Lucy doll a full examination. He said Lucy is doing great!

January 17, 2015

The bitties and I were in the kitchen earlier getting ready to leave.

Sally (6): *Starts sobbing uncontrollably*
Me: What happened?
Sally: I can't find Lucy! I LOST HER!
Eric (8): It's a doll.
Me: Honey, she's not lost. She's here. She probably crawled off exploring and is playing somewhere. It's okay. Let's look for her. Make sure she's not getting into anything she shouldn't.
Eric: It's a doll!
Sally: Ok
Sally and I go into living room to look.
Me: She's probably hiding your crayons again.
Eric: *From the kitchen* A DOLL!
Me: Find your crayons, and you'll probably find Lucy.
Sally: OK *Heads upstairs*
Eric: MOM! IT'S A DOLL!

Sally: *Coming downstairs* You were right!
Me: You find her?
Sally: Yeah, she was coloring in my room.
Eric: Are you kidding me?!
Me: Good. Glad you found her.
Eric: I can't believe this. It's. A. Doll.
Sally: She was like this. *Demonstrates exactly how she found Lucy sitting and coloring.*
Me: She likes to color like her mama.
Eric: *Muttering more to himself* UGH! A doll! It's a doll people! I can't believe they're talking about a doll. A DOLL!

February 13, 2015

I spent 26 minutes on hold with Disney World because Sally (6) needed to ask questions about Lucy Doll. I explained to the customer service rep that I assured Sally dolls were allowed in the parks, and

I'm sure many children bring them. Sally wanted to make sure Lucy could go on the rides with her. The rep explained that Lucy Doll is definitely most welcome on the rides, just make sure she's buckled in tight. Gauging the tone of voice at the start of the call and how it changed with her reactions to the questions, I think we just made that woman's day.

February 16, 2015

Earlier this evening, dinner was just about ready when Sally (6) made a mad dash out the back door. I thought man! The dog got out! Then Griffin ran in front of me. Eric (8) looked out the back door, turned to me and asked what happened because Sally just took off. I told him I had no idea. Eric took off after Sally while I still had two pans going on the stove and food to take out of the oven. After a couple minutes, I could go check on them. (Mind you, I could hear them through the kitchen window, so I knew they were by the back door.)

Before going outside, I could already hear the crying through the kitchen window. Sally was upset, and I could hear Eric talking to her.

I get outside, and Sally is bawling. Eric had one arm around her telling her that it'll be okay, and he's sure I will take them in the car to look.

I ask what's wrong, and Sally wails that Lucy is gone.

Me: What do you mean she's gone?
Sally (6): I left her outside.
Me: No.
Sally: Yes! I left her outside in her stroller,

and the wind blew her away.

Me: Come inside.

Sally: We have to go find her!!

Me: My car keys are inside. So are your shoes. Come inside.

Once inside, I pointed near the table.

Me: Honey, you put Lucy in her high chair when you started helping me cook, and her stroller is in the living room.

Poor Sally!! She was heartbroken!

April 15, 2015

Sally (6) tagged along with Eric (8) when he went to his friend Konner's house. She brought Lucy with her. Of course. When they came home, Sally told me that Konner made fun of her for having a baby doll.

Me: *to Eric* What did you do?

Eric: What?

Me: Did you tell him to stop?

Eric: Yeah. *to Sally* Didn't I? I told him not to make fun of her for Lucy, and that Sally really loves Lucy.

Sally: Yeah.

Eric: But Sally was already upset, and Konner said she was whining like a baby. And I was mad. I told him that she was only crying because he made fun of her, and he better stop it.

Me: *beaming* Did he stop?

Eric and Sally: Yeah.

Me: *to Eric* How you act will always be more important to me than how someone else acts.

April 17, 2015

Going to bed. I gave Lucy a few bites of 3 Musketeers, and she went hyper all over the living room for a bit. Crazy baby. Just think about my enabling antics for a moment. ... Smiling? Good.

April 17, 2015

The Lucy Doll Chronicles

Sally (6) came home and looked for Lucy asking what Lucy did all day like she always does. Eric (8) is annoyed by the idea that Lucy does anything at all given that she's a doll as he always is.

Sally: Did she hide my crayons again?
Me: No. I kept her from the crayons.
Sally: Good! She's hidden almost all of them.
Eric: She doesn't hide anything.
Sally: Yes, she does. What did she do today?
Me: She played in her swing, crawled up

to your room...

Sally: I hope she didn't make a mess.

Eric: She can't do anything. She's a doll.

Sally: Yes, she can Eric!

Eric: You do realize Lucy can't move anywhere? The only reason she moves around while we're gone is because mom picks her up and moves her.

Sally: Well of course mom moved her. Lucy is just a baby. She can't walk!

May 6, 2015

I noticed Lucy doll on the kitchen table late last night. I figured Sally would be upset in the morning to realize she left Lucy all night. Lucy stayed with me. In the morning, Sally asked me why I had Lucy. I told her because she was in the kitchen when I was headed to bed. Sally rolled her eyes and said, "She was probably looking for a treat. I always catch her in there

looking for cookies or cake or something!"
May 21, 2015

I walked to the bus stop this afternoon carrying Lucy. Carmen's grandma said, "Oh I see you had your baby!" I cradled Lucy, and told all the ladies what a good and quiet baby Lucy is.

The bus comes around the corner, and I'm holding Lucy where she will be highly visible. Sally gets off the bus first and comes running like she always does. She gets a foot from me before she finally sees Lucy. Sally's eyes widen, she yells "LUCY!", and scoops her up. Sally spins her around just like a scene out of Hollywood.

Sally (6): *gives me a great big hug* Thank you, mom!

Me: You're welcome, baby.

Eric walks up.

Eric (8): *very disappointed* You found Lucy.

Me: Yes.

Eric: ... Did you have to?

May 27, 2015

Talking Halloween costumes...

Sally (6): What's Lucy going to be?

Me: I don't know...

Sally: We have to find something for Lucy to be for Halloween!

Eric (9): A doll?

October 23, 2015

The Children's Church cast roles today for the Nativity play. Sally was given the roles of Mary and an angel. Lucy, you ask? Lucy

will play baby Jesus.
November 29, 2015

I put a gift for Sally under the tree. She gives it a quick shake, makes a quick guess, then forgets about it.

I put a gift for Lucy under the tree. Sally closely inspects it then follows me from room to room the rest of the night demanding to know what it is. She cracks me up.

Yes, I buy a Christmas gift for Lucy every year. Don't judge me. Family is family. Doesn't matter if you're blood or not. Doesn't matter if you're a doll.
December 21, 2016

Chapter 9
Bitty Dictionary

Bitty Dictionary: "I don't know"

We've all been there. You walk in a room, and see a new red mural that you didn't commission on your wall. Your child has red marker all over his/her hands, but when you ask, "Who did this?" Your child responds, "I don't know."

This "lie" only infuriates you further. Please know, your child is not saying, "I don't know who did this." Your child is ACTUALLY saying, "I don't know what the punishment is, so I'm not sure if I should confess or hire a lawyer because I don't think I can survive bitty jail."

Next time, try a new angle. When you see the new mural simply say, "That's beautiful. Is it a ducky?" When your child replies, "No, mommy, it's a doggie. I made it 'specially for you", you now have a full confession which means you can skip the jury of their peers.

Straight to bitty jail. Do not pass go. Do not collect $200.

January 5, 2015

Bitty Wisdom

Sally (6) was playing a board game. She turned the board over, and there's a picture covering the other side.

Sally: Look!
Me: *looks* Cool.

Sally: I made this.

Me: *knowing she didn't* Wow! You ARE talented.

Sally: No, I didn't. Never trust a girl who plays games.

Me: *slow building laugh as I thought about what she said*

Sally: And all girls play games!

Me: *full on cackle*

March 14, 2015

Mini Dictionary Vol. 1 (AKA The World According to Eric)

Staging - (verb)
The act of standing on a stage, and then you "ing!"
July 2, 2016

I do not fully understand bitty vocabulary,

and I wish I had a bitty dictionary.

"Hold on." ~ Continue to do, say, eat, drink, go, etc. whatever it was you were asking to do to begin with because apparently being told you must ask first doesn't imply you must also receive an affirmative answer.

"Hold on; I have to go to the bathroom." ~ Continue the conversation from the other side of the bathroom door.

Yet...

"Hold on while I get dessert or other treat ready, get the movie started, or other assorted fun preparation taken care of." ~ Sit perfectly still like little angels without movement or noise.

January 3, 2015

You know how you count between lightning strikes and thunder to tell how far away the storm is?

Well, the same trick applies to a child's accident. The sooner the cry, the worse the injury. They fall and see blood, immediate cry. They hit hard and it hurts, immediate cry. They fall and take stock of their body, seeing/feeling no injury, then cry anyway because it scared them.

Sally (6) tried on Eric's (8) wheelie shoes.

Eric: I got you... I got you... I DON'T GO... *screams* MOM!
Me: "One Hippopotamus. Two Hippopotamus. Three"
Sally: *cries*
Me: *And we're good!"
January 18, 2015

Chapter 10
Misc.

I came home to quiet. The kids were off playing nicely together. No yelling or arguing. The toys were all picked up and not a dish in the sink. There wasn't even a trail of book bags, shoes, and coats marking their entrance into the house from the school bus. Suddenly panic set in as I realized I was in the wrong house!
February 22, 2013

How to guarantee everyone in your home is awake in the middle of the night for at least two hours:

1. Hear a noise that alerts you a child has

woken up and is up to no good.

2. Investigate.

3. Confiscate can of Mountain Dew your child took from the refrigerator.

4. Toss can on your bed for safe keeping while you put your child back to bed.

5. Go off to do random other things while you're up completely forgetting there is a very cold can of pop on the sheet of your bed.

6. Go to bed already; it's 1 in the morning!

7. Enter bedroom, turn off light, and lay down.

8. Lay down in a manner that the freezing cold can of pop hits right in the back of your knee.

9. Scream like the wrath of Khan is upon you.

10. Spend the next two hours comforting the children you woke from a dead sleep and putting them back to bed.

Life is good.
September 3, 2014

One of life's many conundrums is that when my children are out of the home, my thermometers will no longer be played with and broken or lost. However, when my children are out of the home, I will have a drastic reduction in the need for a thermometer.
October 31, 2014

Eric (8) stirs in his sleep, and I hear him speak. Not sure if he woke up, or if he's talking in his sleep.

Me: You okay, baby?
Eric: Oh, that's creepy.
Me: *figure he's sleep talking* What's creepy?

Eric: The thing that puts you back together.

Me: What thing that puts you back together?

Eric: Ohhhhh just something I think of after a while.

Me: ....

Me: ....

Me: ....

Me: Eric, are you asleep?

Eric: Yeah, mom. Go back to bed.

November 10, 2014

Eric (8): Mom, one of our spelling words is "comfortable", and I had to use it. I said, "Comfortable is snuggling up with a hot cup of cocoa and watching Supernatural."

Me: Um hmm what did your teacher say?

Eric: She asked what Supernatural was, and I told her it was a deadly show.

Me: Um hmm... Is she calling or emailing?

Eric: *looks surprised* Huh?! Emailing! How'd you know?
November 10, 2014

Doing some light housework, I start singing "Blueberry Hill". My kids leave the room. I laughed and asked if they don't like my singing. (I can't carry a tune in a bucket.)

Eric (8): You're a great singer! (This one is gonna be a great man someday.)
Sally (6): You always make stuff up and sing it. *groans*
Me: *alarmed by the statement!*

So, I put on some Fats Domino, and now there are three bopping around doing housework.
November 22, 2014

I just taught my bitties how to tell if a 9V battery still has juice. Forget their toys, a 9V is their new favorite game to play.
December 19, 2014

OMG! Someone report me! I wouldn't let him play on the tablet. THEN I wouldn't let him have a piece of candy. Worst mom ever!!
January 4, 2015

The bitties caught a cicada yesterday at my brother's. Brought it home in a coffee can.

Guess what happened to this mama at 5:30 in the morning in a dark house when she woke up and went to start her day?

The house is still standing. The kitchen

may need some work though. And my throat is raw. I'll leave the details to your imagination.

July 17, 2015

Eric (9): Why do you call your slippers "footies"?
Me: *shrugs* I don't know. Why do I call you two bitties?
Eric: Because we're bitty.
Sally (6): Well...they're footy.

July 25, 2015

Me: Eric, I will give you ... FIVE imaginary dollars if you do something for me.
Eric (8): What? No!
Me: No?
Eric: Not for imaginary dollars.
Me: Why not?
Eric: Because it's not REAL dollars!

A few minutes later...

Me: Eric?

Eric: No.

Me: What no?

Eric: I'm not doing anything for imaginary dollars.

Me: You don't even know what I want you to do.

Eric: Doesn't matter. I'm not doing it for imaginary dollars.

Me: More than I usually pay you.

Eric: What? Nuh-uh!

Me: I usually pay you no dollars. Imaginary dollars is more than no dollars.

Eric: Mom ... *shakes head*

A few minutes later...

Me: Eric?

Eric: No. Sally can do it.

Sally (6): No, I'm NOT doing it.

Me: Why not? Neither of you even know what I want you to do.

Sally: Not for five imaginary dollars. Maybe for twenty imaginary dollars.

Me: Sorry. I don't have that much.

Eric: MOM!!

Me: What?

Eric: How could you not have twenty imaginary dollars? They're IMAGINARY.

Me: My imagination isn't that rich.

Eric: *smiles* Mom, I love you.

July 28, 2015

About the Author

Jenn Williams is a writer which seems rather obvious considering this is an about the author bio. When it comes to writing, there are no bounds to her creativity and ideas. She is a mother of 3 from central Illinois. She enjoys spending time with her children and granddaughter, writing, and entertaining friends and family with her comedic wit.

Jenn lives in a house which she prefers over living in a car. Something about confined space and indoor plumbing. She is quite sarchotic walking the fine line between sarcasm and crazy. Jenn believes there is no problem that can't be solved with chocolate or bacon.

When she is not writing, Jenn spends her

time refereeing her two younger children and napping. There is never a bad time for a nap. She also enjoys cooking, animals, nature and spending time with her main squeeze, Netflix. That's "cooking (comma) animals" not "cooking animals." Although, both would be accurate.

www.ingramcontent.com/pod-product-compliance
Lightning Source LLC
Chambersburg PA
CBHW030332100526
44592CB00010B/666